CW00376493

PHOTOGRAPHS
GERED MANKOWITZ *(pages 6, 7, 85, 96)*
BARRY MARSDEN *(pages 54, 62)*
PAUL SLATTERY *(pages 1, 26, 27, 31, 34, 35, 38, 39, 42, 43, 45, 46, 47, 58, 68, 71, 72, 73, 74, 75, 78, 79, 82, 83, 86, 87, 88, 89, 90, 91, 94, 95)*
© **CAMERAPRESS** *(pages 50, 51, 52)*
© **REDFERNS** *(pages 17, 24, 28, 36, 37, 40, 41, 44, 60, 64, 76, 77, 92)*
© **RETNA PICTURES LTD** *(pages 3, 4, 9, 10, 11, 12, 14, 16, 19, 20, 21, 22, 23, 66 , 80, 81, 84)*
© **REX FEATURES** *(pages 32, 33, 48, 53, 56, 57, 93)*

TEXT BY JEMMA WHEELER
EDITED BY DANIEL PATTON

THIS EDITION PUBLISHED IN 1995 BY
VINYL EXPERIENCE LTD, LONDON, ENGLAND.

how does it feel?

by Jemma Wheeler

There are few bands who live up to their hype. ery now and then there is a glimmer of brilliance the mire of one hit wonders. Oasis are that ining light. Their history is a brief but intense e. In eighteen months they have gone from ing nobodies to being the most talked about nd since The Stone Roses and the most credible orking class band since the Happy Mondays. eir name has become synonymous with success d excess, with rock 'n' roll, debauchery and the ee minute pop song.

Before their arrival, the British music industry d reached a point of stagnation - everything had en done. Even dance music, seemingly the iour of pop had run out of ideas. Oasis have en the music industry renewed confidence in f, reminding us just how important British sic is, and they have done so without the nostalgic overtones of style and content so beloved of other contemporary bands. They have done this by having confidence in themselves, by making music purely because they think it's brilliant. Oasis demand to have a book written about them and I'm sure there will be many more in the future, because the important things that Oasis offer are impact, longevity and straight-forward talent.

Oasis in their larval form were a rather disastrous band called The Rain, coming from Burnage, a suburb of Manchester. They consisted of four bored men: Paul 'Bonehead' Arthurs (Guitar); Paul 'Guigs' McGuigan (Bass); Tony McCarroll (Drums) and a singer who was soon ousted to make way for the 21 year old Liam Gallagher. Changing their name to Oasis was the easy part. Writing some decent songs was a completely different ball game.

At that time, Noel Gallagher, a self-taught guitarist who had been playing since he was 13, was working as a road technician for the Inspiral Carpets. He had just returned home from a long and arduous American tour to be faced with hearing his little brother's new band. His reaction was simple. He told Liam in no uncertain terms that although they looked good, their songs were 'shite', but that if they let him join and write the songs they might just get somewhere. He was a tough negotiator. As he told Mark Ellen of Mojo magazine, he said to them: "If I join this band - and I mean it right - you fucking belong to me seven days a week and we rehearse six nights a week and we're going for it big time."

The rest of this story is a series of right place, right time situations. After a lot of hard work and brotherly tension, in July of 1993 Oasis had put together a demo tape which miraculously fell in the hands of one Johnny Marr. The story goes th Noel met up with an old mate called Ian, who used to know from his days hanging out in th Hacienda Club. Ian asked Noel for a copy of H demo 'to play to our kid'. Noel had with him recently purchased copy of The The's *Dusk* LP a Ian commented on how pleased his kid was w it. Suddenly Noel clicked: "Who the fuck's yc kid?" The 'kid' in question was Johnny Marr.

History was made. Johnny liked the tape a phoned Noel within a few hours of hearing it. asked Noel what guitars he played and Noel te him about his tobacco brown 1970 Epipho Riviera purchased in a vintage guitar shop

Oasis are (L-
Tony McCarroll (Drums), Paul 'Bonehead' Arth
(Guitar), Liam Gallagher (vocals), Paul 'Gu
McGuigan (Bass), Noel Gallagher (Guit

Liam in the driving seat

oncaster. Johnny Marr was so excited about the
scovery of a new vintage guitar shop that he drove
m over there the next day. Noel, who was on the
le at the time stood and watched Johnny spend
,500 on guitars. If he hadn't known before, Noel
ew then exactly what he wanted out of life. Soon
er, Johnny's manager Marcus Russell signed Oasis
er seeing them play only six songs in a support
t for Dodgy. Johnny Marr got on so well with
el that he even gave him the Gibson Les Paul
tar he wrote *The Queen is Dead* on (it was
ginally owned by Pete Townshend). After Noel
ed it at someone's head, he rather cheekily
mplained to Johnny that it didn't sound too good
could really do with repairing, Johnny sent
nd another with a note saying: "You'll like this
, it's a lot heavier and will fracture anybody's
l if you get a good swing on it..."

August 1993: Oasis are booked to play an
opening set for long forgotten Creation signing,
Boyfriend in Glasgow. They also discover that
Creation boss, Alan McGee will be in attendance.
They arrive at the venue and apparently no one
there knows anything about them. A lot of threats
later, they are allowed to play a four song set
before the venue opens. With the luck of the devil
McGee turns up early to the show and catches the
band's short set. McGee's reaction is fast and
positive; this is the band he had been waiting for
since he set up Creation ten years ago. By the time
Oasis saunter off stage, he is waiting to negotiate a
deal with them. Without the usual inertia of an
A&R department to contend with, the deal is
established in record time.

McGee had no doubt how much he wanted
Oasis. In his opinion, seeing them that night

could only be compared to seeing the Rolling Stones during the adolescent stage of their career. He described them as "brutal, exciting and arrogant." A world-wide distribution deal with Sony made sure the band would be very comfortable for a long time to come. By the November of that year Oasis are filling support slots for some of the biggest indie names of that time: Saint Etienne; Verve and Liz Phair are among those they open for, always making a huge impression on audiences who are usually not very receptive to support bands. By the time December comes around they have already begun work on their debut album. Creation install them in the famous Mono Valley Studios in Monmouth, South Wales. One day while wandering around Monmouth, Noel bumps into Ian Brown of the Stone Roses, who are also recording at the time.

Gift of the gob

Ian expresses his approval of Oasis to Noel. Two days later, a label representative turns up to make a progress report. All he finds is a £600 drink and drugs bill and some rough recordings of Rolling Stones songs with Noel singing. Eventually they get it together. Eighteen or twenty tracks are recorded and by the spring of 1994 they basically have everything in the bag and ready to go. This allows them to concentrate on touring and building up their name and reputation without any of the pressure of recording hanging over their heads.

When, in the January, Creation organise a secret invite-only gig at Kings Cross Splash Club, two hundred people have to be turned away at the door. Already their reputation is getting out of control. On the return journey from supporting

Going Manc again

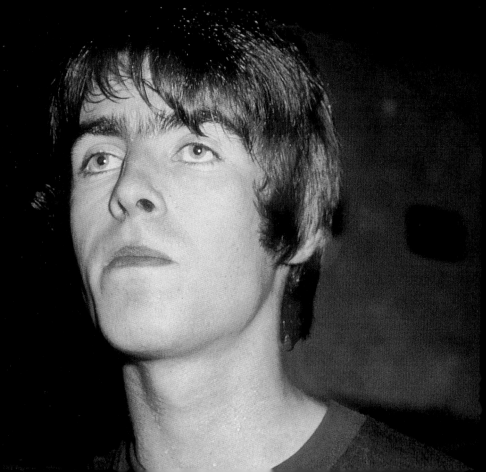

left:

Mr Lippy in rare tight-lipped pose

right:

Feeling Supersonic

left:
Oasis on 'The Word'

right:
Shake, rattle and stroll

Verve in Amsterdam, all the band members except Noel are arrested for fighting and vandalising furniture. Next up comes a co-headline tour with Whiteout. Although they are meant to swap the headline position each night Oasis begin as headliners and continue every night. This tour included the infamous sell out London show at the 100 Club where Glaswegian boys Whiteout could not help but admit, Oasis blew them off stage. But according to McD, Whiteout's manager, the press stories concerning the tension between the brothers is being blown out of all proportion, and that on-stage fights are merely nasty glares between the brothers.

April 11, 1994: Oasis' debut single *Supersonic* is released. The single is apparently about a nine stone Rottweiller dog called Elsa who was in the

oasis

Creation 'Undrugged'

dio when they recorded it. Seven days later it ters the charts at number 31. Later the same onth the band headline a UK tour. Speed of owth like this is rarely heard of in the indie usic industry. By June they have toured again, d out the Marquee club and appeared at the yal Albert Hall as part of Creation's acoustic thday celebration 'Undrugged'. Their notoriety ows as tales of hotel trashing and sibling fights ckly spread.

he second single *Shakermaker* is released on e 20. Within a week it enters the charts at nber 11. Noel is given the honour of being ited to play guitar with Crazy Horse, Neil ng's legendary band at a gig at London's gs College. By the end of the month, the ht after their performance at Glastonbury,

Oasis have joined that exclusive club belonging only to The Fall and The Mission by getting banned from The Columbia Hotel in London. All this and Top of the Pops.

One week into August and *Live Forever* is released. Oasis embark on yet another sell-out UK tour. At Newcastle Riverside a member of the crowd punches Noel on stage (said man is given a 'right kicking'). Noel refuses to play on. After the show, a mob of three hundred people attack the tour bus and smash its windows as it pulls away. Following in the footsteps of the previous singles, *Live Forever* charts at Number 10 just one week after its release.

Two weeks into August and Oasis have sold out the two thousand capacity London Forum, no mean feat for a band yet to release their first album. After the Forum show, Noel and Paul Weller get chatting back stage. Weller asks Noel what he thought of his last album *Wildwood*. Noel's response is that it had given him something to better. He then says something along the lines of, 'Now get out of my dressing room and tell me I'm God'. Two days later they play yet another sell-out date at London's Astoria.

(continued on page 49)

Noel searches for perfect pitch on tour in Tokyo

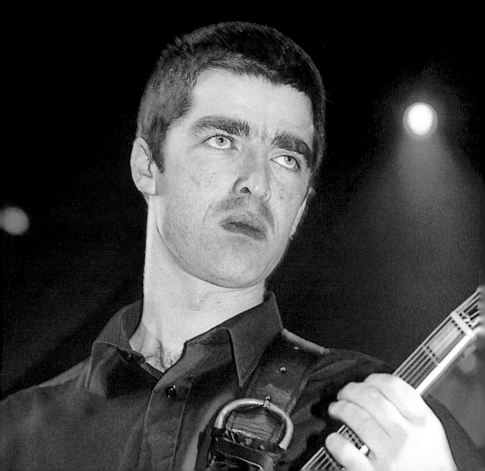

Keeping tabs
Backstage, Providence, USA

Lager Lads
Backstage, TOTP

oasis

Noel unleashes another killer chorus

Baby, I'm a rock 'n' roll star

Noel on Radio 1FM live

Lomax club, Liverp

Brighton Centre

43

how does it feel?

Legendary 100 Club gig
London

oasis

Fleece and Firkin, Bristol

The Venue, New Cross
London

Oasis' debut album *Definitely Maybe* is
eased on August 31, 1994 (apart from in
eden where an inexplicable error from Sony
ans it goes on sale a week early. The first 20
usand copies sell out and disgruntled fans,
able to buy a copy, lay siege to the Sony
ces). Within a week it is confirmed that
finitely Maybe has become the fastest selling
ut album of all time with 150 thousand sales
oss the counter within the first few days of it
ng on sale. A special in-store gig and signing
ion is arranged at London's Marble Arch
ich of the Virgin Megastore. Fans get an extra
ial treat as Lemonheads singer Evan Dando
s the band on stage. By this time Evan has
ome a friend of the band; he has been tagging
g with them since they shared the same bill at
Dutch Lowlands festival (though his

outrageous antics had even them bemused on
occasions). He plays a special acoustic support slot
when Oasis play the Buckley Tivoli. After the show,
Evan decides to serenade the couple of hundred
strong crowd from on top of the venues roof.

Definitely Maybe is an album about fulfilling
your dreams. You can take a line from just about
every track that will illustrate this: "You can have it
all" (*Supersonic*); "These could be the best days of
your life" (*Digsy's Diner*); the list goes on. As the
band have said: if you've been on the dole living in
a rough area, you don't have to sing about it, in fact
you're more likely to sing about more positive
things, about your dreams and how they came
through. *Definitely Maybe* has been criticised for
not having enough depth to stand the test of time,
but what it does undeniably have is pure pop
moments, fused with rock 'n' roll. It is only a debut

Evan Dando lends a hand, at the in-store performance
Virgin Megastore, Marble Arch, London

Mr Tambourine

Dazed and conf

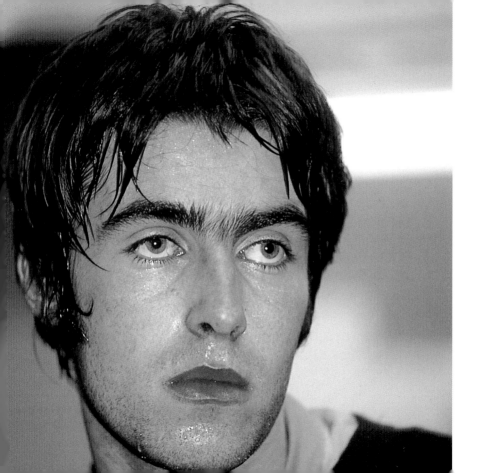

bum and few debut albums have ever had this any perfect moments. Definitely Maybe offers a ozen reasons why Oasis are the best band of the oment. They combine pop and rock in a way not ossible without melting down *Revolver* and *Exile* in *Main Street* and making them one record.

The summer of '94 saw Oasis braving the allenge that is America during (but not a part of y 'industry circus' as Noel put it) the New Music minar in New York. By the September they were aying in LA: a reporter from the LA Daily News otted Ringo Starr and his wife outside the Oasis ow at Whiskey A Go Go's. The LA show was one Oasis' few bad gigs but, if the stories of what y had been getting up to during their stay are ything to go by, it was hardly surprising. The nd had been really going for it, LA style.

Oasis arrive at the infamous Viper Room (the club where the Chilli Peppers hang out, and River Phoenix had his last dance) at 2am when the club likes to close. They refuse to finish their beers and leave. Predictable as ever, there's a scuffle, though probably not up to much by LA standards. They then proceed to party until 6am at Bonehead's brother's house. As the sun comes up, Bonehead is to be found in the middle of the street fully equipped, playing *Supersonic* over and over until the full force of the LAPD arrive. Shades, attitude, squad cars and a reputation to live up to. Bonehead is told to stop playing and come quietly. After this, Oasis could hardly be expected to play a stormer.

In late September Oasis fly to Japan for a short tour. The dates sell out the day they are announced, even though they have not had a record released there yet. Throughout their stay in

oasis

"I need to be myself"

Shades of rhythm

Japan, the band are mobbed by Japanese girls wearing Manchester City Shirts. They are inundated with presents, some outrageously expensive, some just plain weird. Everything from footballs to rare Beatles bootlegs. Their last night in Tokyo is only Oasis' 100th gig ever. At the final night in Nagoya they perform their first encore.

October 17th: *Cigarettes & Alcohol* is released, a song that Noel admits was really just a piss-take that everybody liked. In December Oasis are ready to put in their bid for the Christmas number one. On December 12th, *Whatever* with its orchestral parts and lyrics that bask in the glory of being whoever you want and doing whatever you want makes it to number 3 in the charts a week after its release. Appearances on Top of the Pops (again) and Later With Jools Holland make sure everyone

The Cresten Hotel, Nagoya

is humming the single over the Christmas period and beyond. Bridging generation gaps thought impossible in this day and age, *Whatever* summed up an amazing year for Oasis. A single every three months and a record breaking album. And this is only the beginning.

However successful you become, motivation can always be a problem. Like any young band it's hard to concentrate, difficult not to lose sight of what is really important whilst being carried away on some rock 'n' roll whirlwind. Noel admits that there were times when it was very difficult to keep the rest of the band motivated. As he told Mark Ellen: "Nobody was taking any notice of us and they were like, 'I'm not going to rehearse, what's the point? You're just acting like we're the fucking Beatles.' And it came right in the end. Now I can stand there and say I told you so."

Oasis' career is a long line of sell out shows, hit
gles, fights, Top of the Pops appearances and
er major successes, all punctuated by brotherly
e and tension. In conversation with Cliff Jones of
e Face Noel said: "Liam's young, he's on a
mplete trip and he's all mouth at the moment.
's a genius frontman and was born to do this.
he also wishes he was me. Always has done."
m, of course, sees it completely differently: "I
w he's talking shite, so don't gimme none of
brotherly love bollocks. He's a sad twat who
ts to jam with a load of old men. And I'm not."
here have been many tempestuous
tionships in the history of rock: Morrissey and
r; Reed and Cale. Townshend and Daltrey of
Who are especially relevant as Pete
nshend, like Noel, wrote all the songs then

herly tug

stood back and played guitar watching Roger
Daltrey sing them. There have also been many
brother musical partnerships, many of which have
never run smoothly: William and Jim Reid of the
Jesus and Mary Chain have never held back on
expressing their feelings; Ray and Dave Davies of
The Kinks have been known to stay in different
hotels whilst on tour together and Phil and Don
Everly who split up in true rock 'n' roll style whilst
on stage in 1973, Phil ceremoniously smashing
his guitar and Don declaring that the Everly
Brothers died ten years ago. It doesn't take family
ties to make people squabble, but it does make
good copy. There's one tale that tells how Noel
and Liam didn't talk to each other for two weeks
after a punch up in New York when Noel refused
to pass Liam a beer. But at the bottom of it all
there still seems to be a closeness between the

Gallagher brothers that only brothers can really share. Not that they'd ever admit it of course. Noel says that the closest they have ever got was when Liam said: "I wouldn't sing anyone else's songs but yours and John Lennon's." And Noel replied: "I wouldn't have anyone else sing my songs but you and John Lennon."

Rock 'n' roll debauchery has always been a winner when it comes to selling bucket loads of records. Believe it or not there are still thousands of no-life people out there who read these stories and think *cool, I wish I could be like that* and proceed to live their lives through the adventures of other, braver and more famous souls. But it doesn't take long to see through the tales. Any band can get famous for smashing up hotels, but Oasis have more than that. Although their story is littered with tales of drugs, violence, hotel

molition, groupies, drunkenness, mindless
ɔlence and a bit more hotel trashing, Liam
nies being a hooligan. He told Cliff Jones of The
ce: "I'm aggressive but I'm no fucking hooligan,
 no Evan Dando either, all this 'I do smack, I do
ck', fucking tortured artist bit. I admit it, I love
ɔrting, I love sex, but I'm not into smashing
ngs up. Chairs are for sitting on in my book."

n comparison, guitarist Bonehead has
:ome something of a world-class hotel
ecker; he could smash furniture for England,
ʻmpic level. Admitting his talent to The Face,
h just a little irony he says: "I tell 'em it takes
rs of practice to get this good. I've got a chair
ny house that I practice throwing out of the
dow." Noel puts it all down to the other
d members simply getting bored. After all,

he's got writing music to keep him occupied
during the tedious moments of long periods
away from home.

Liam's fiery temperament has been bated by
fans many times: their habit of insulting
Manchester City as he walks on stage, or throwing
bottles has always been a success when it comes
to pissing Liam off beyond all comprehension.
During a performance at the Heineken Festival,
Liam cut the set dead and said: "We wanna
fucking play for you lot, so don't start. We're not
fucking dickheads and we're not Blur."

The fact is people wind Liam up because it's just
too easy. He has yet to realise that if he just ignores
them they'll soon get bored, but until then, they'll
just keep on going. Liam's quick-fire retaliation is
typical of the way people react when they become

y famous, very quickly. They are not used to the ention and although Liam is seen to wallow in he is probably only just adjusting to it. Of urse another reason is that as he's said, he's just prepared to play in front of philistines, and that ey prevent him from becoming absorbed in the sic, they just don't deserve to hear the songs.

Oasis are more than just musicians; they tomise something about today's culture. They real people who genuinely believe in what they doing. Musically they are never afraid of the vious and have been accused of simply ripping old songs and melodies, but they quite rightly n't see it like that, as Noel told Mark Ellen: ere's twelve notes and thirty six chords. All figurations have been done and that's the end of

atever' video shoot (pages 68-74)

it." When the similarity of *Cigarettes and Alcohol* to T Rex is mentioned he laughs: "The whole song is a joke. I was laughing to meself when I wrote it. The whole thing was meant to be ironic."

The Oasis theory is based around the idea that if you don't want to be as big as the Beatles, then it's just a hobby. It's been 30 years since the Beatles' first number 1 and we are expected to have progressed from the simple appeal of an electric guitar and a voice. By definition something better should exist. Oasis prove that this does not have to be so, but then they are about much more than music. Oasis are about style, not style in the obvious sense but style in a broader sense than many of the generic bands of today aspire to. Oasis look cool without even trying. Guigs describes this as a Manchester

ning, commenting on how even if a player for Manchester City scores ten goals in a season, if he doesn't look good in the kit, the fans will hate him. Oasis are cool because they make looking cool so easy.

Oasis can be accused of being old fashioned; their music can be compared to that of the Beatles, T Rex, and the Rolling Stones, but they still say something about today's society. They are a genuine product of the 1990's; five working-class lads from Manchester who set their hearts on doing something and did all they could to get it. The 80's and 90's are the time of Generation X, of the slacker generation who aspire to doing nothing because there is nothing worth doing, of people who live in the past or in day dreams because they believe the future holds nothing for them. Oasis go against all of this. They have proved that there is hope in the here and now, that this is a time for rock 'n' roll and three minute pop songs about having a good time, as much as it's about chemical stimulants and dancing to repetitive beats all night. They prove that there's a space for anything as long as it's good and genuine. Oasis have made pop matter again. Noel Gallagher claims that the material for the second album is already written. I believe him. Oasis are the band we've been waiting for, the band we all needed. And most of all they're the band of the future.

Anyone fancy a game of footie?

Glastonbury Festival, '94

Cigarette & alcohol
Glastonbury, 94

oasis

left:
Let me take you down...
Green Oasis, NYC

right:
Backstage at Glastonbury
with the Inspiral Carpets

oasis

Johnny Marr gave me this

Wetlands, NY

Watch and learn

Are you looking at me?
Noel in Osaka

oasis

Le Palais,
Hammersmith, London,
Dec '94

Noel slides away

Turning Japanese
Nagoya, September '94

Liam: "I've always sung me cock

oasis

First we take Manhattan

Noel on Broadway, NYC

Scorn In the USA
Liam on 5th Avenue, NYC